Taking Responsibility
The Rural Environment

The Environmental Agenda

Taking Responsibility
Promoting Sustainable Practice through Higher Education Curricula

Programme Coordinator
Shirley Ali Khan, Council for Environmental Education

Series Editors
Sally Richardson, WWF UK (World Wide Fund for Nature)
Shirley Ali Khan, Environmental Responsibility Centre,
University of Hertfordshire

The Environmental Agenda

Taking Responsibility
The Rural Environment

Written and compiled by
Shirley Ali Khan, *University of Hertfordshire*

In association with John Peters, University of Reading
Research: Susan Rabbich and Adria Pittock,
　Farmers World Network National Agricultural Centre

*A Council for Environmental Education Programme funded by the
Department of the Environment, in partnership with WWF (UK)*

Pluto Press

LONDON · EAST HAVEN, CT
in association with WWF UK

First published 1995 by Pluto Press
345 Archway Road, London N6 5AA
and 140 Commerce Street,
East Haven, CT 06512, USA

British Library Cataloguing in Publication Data
A catalogue record for this book is available from the British Library

ISBN 0 7453 0935 6 Paperback

Taking Responsibility titles appear in The Environmental Agenda series
published by Pluto Press in association with WWF UK.
ISSN 1353 – 6842

99   98   97   96   95
 5   4   3   2   1

Designed and produced for Pluto Press by
Chase Production Services, Chipping Norton, OX7 5QR
Typeset from author's disks by Stanford DTP Services, Milton Keynes
Printed on recycled paper in the EC by JW Arrowsmith Ltd

Contents

PREFACE

This publication is one of a series produced as part of the Council for Environmental Education's Education and Training for Business and the Environment programme. The broad aim of the programme is to develop environmental education policy and practice within the further and higher education sector, with a particular focus on the needs of business and industry.

The programme is supported by the Department of the Environment and the World Wide Fund for Nature (WWF UK) and stems from the government's commitment in the 1990 White Paper 'This Common Inheritance' to sponsor a series of conferences with a 'market place' function, bringing together industry, educationalists, trainers and course providers.

The publication series is the outcome of a national series of seminars, which took place between March 1993 and January 1994, and an associated national research exercise to identify appropriate environmental content, skills and good practice relating to integration and evaluation methods in eleven targeted educational areas.

This publication is based on the research material drawn in by the University of Reading's Centre for Agricultural Strategy, the Farmers World Network and the University of Hertfordshire's Environmental Responsibility Centre. Reading University also hosted the national seminar on the theme Environmental Education through Higher Education Curricula: the Rural Environment.

CONTEXT

1.1   Key Concepts

Sustainability

> There are many dimensions to sustainability. First it requires the elimination of poverty and deprivation. Second it requires the conservation and enhancement of the resource base which alone can ensure that the elimination of poverty is permanent. Third, it requires a broadening of the concept of development so that it covers not only economic growth but also social and cultural development. Fourth, and most important, it requires the unification of economics and ecology in decision making at all levels. (Prime Minister Gro Harlem Brundtland, Sir Peter Scott lecture, Bristol, 8 October 1986)

A society pursuing sustainability should reflect this concept centrally in its education system.

Whole institution response

A whole institution response to environmental concerns requires all areas of institutional activity to take account of the environment. Setting the institution's curriculum in its appropriate environmental context will not be credible if institutional practice is unsustainable. All members of an institution, from principal to student, are required to play a part in a whole institution response to environmental concerns.

Environmental education for all

Environmental education for all is the integration of appropriate environmental elements across higher education curricula, the purpose being to set work and everyday life in a sustainable context. The process is also referred to as 'cross-curricular greening'. Cross-curricular greening provision has two strands which overlap to some extent:

i.   Environmental education for personal and social responsibility: this includes an appreciation of the forces which determine human attitudes and behaviour towards the environment and of how students' own lifestyles impact on the environment, both locally and globally, together with the development of appropriate personal and practical skills.

ii.   Environmental education for occupational responsibility: this includes an appreciation of the way chosen subjects and vocations connect with, and impact on, the environment, both locally and globally, together with the development of appropriate personal and practical skills.

Both the above areas of provision are specific as opposed to specialised. Students of an environmentally contextualised curriculum would be regarded as specialists in their own right, for example, architects, economists, engineers, horticulturalists, and not as environmental specialists.

Clearly, some subjects and vocations have more connections with the environment than others. For example, land-based courses have significant associated environmental impacts and should therefore contain a significant environmental education component. In contrast, music students would require little or no environmental education relating to their subject.

However, all students, whatever their course, make personal decisions which affect the environment. As such all students require environmental education for personal and social responsibility.

1.2   The Rural Sector and the Environmental Challenge

Impacts
It is important to note that rural sector activity, for example, agriculture, horticulture and forestry and their supporting industries and services, should not have to carry the sole blame for environmental degradation. Many working within the rural sector have a sense of stewardship, and are actively working to restore the environmental integrity of the land through a whole range of measures. However, these measures are not sufficient to off-set the damaging environmental impacts of rural sector activity, many of them dictated by distant agribusiness directors which are far reaching.

For example, the production and use of agrochemicals result in air and water pollution, habitat destruction, loss of visual amenity, contamination of food and fodder and associated damage to animal and human health. Because people are exposed to a cocktail of chemicals in the course of their everyday lives through the air they breathe, the water they drink, the food they eat and the work they do, it is difficult to establish cause and effect of individual chemicals, and even more difficult to identify damaging synergistic effects. Nevertheless it is generally agreed that the diseases of twentieth century living, including cancers of various types and allergies, have environmental connections. The effects of agrochemicals on laboratory animals are easier to measure and draw attention to challenging ethical issues.

A recent research report by the International Institute for Environment and Development (IIED) (Pretty & Howes, 1993) suggested that 'rural culture in Britain would now appear to be as fragile as any in the poor countries of the Third World'. The increased use of external inputs, associated with the intensification and specialisation of agriculture, has resulted in larger farms worked by fewer people. Poor employment opportunities have, in turn, led to the steady decline of rural services and community life. The plight of farmers and farm workers was highlighted in a recent report by the Duke of Westminster in 1992: 'Hidden in the rural landscape which the British so much love, people are suffering poverty, housing problems, unemployment, deprivation of various kinds, and misery ...'

There is also the issue of people's duties and obligations to other species. Such ethical considerations tend to be forgotten in the push towards increased productivity. Causes for concern include painful slaughter, selective breeding techniques, confinement, live transportation, rich diets and the use of growth promoting hormones.

The above examples are indicative of the environment-related issues for the rural sector. A fuller list is given below.

Environmental agenda for the rural sector

i. Ecological Issues

- the loss of local species and varieties of plants and animals due to the maximisation of production through high yielding, disease resistant, artificially engineered species;
- wet-land drainage and ancient woodland clearance to bring more land into production;
- hedgerow destruction to create larger fields for the convenient and profitable operation of large machinery;
- habitat destruction relating to methods of animal grazing and forestry;
- agrochemical run-off into water courses and its effects on aquatic life and surrounding habitats;
- emissions and accidents associated with the agrochemicals industry and their effects;
- secondary pollution effects due to synergy with other chemicals;
- soil erosion and salinisation associated with high-tech farming methods;
- soil impoverishment due to lack of organic returns;
- the depletion of the non-renewable resource base and effects of global warming, acid rain, photochemical smog associated with fossil fuel use for heating and transport:

ii. Ethical Issues

- animal rights in relation to meat eating, animal testing and animal husbandry, transportation and slaughter;
- the impact of transnational chemical companies on local environments and local livelihoods;
- trading practices with Third World countries;
- biotechnology and genetic engineering;
- food surpluses;
- the generation of demand for products.

iii. Health Issues

- effects of agrochemicals on users and local communities, for example, spray drift;
- effects of agrochemical run-off on drinking water quality;
- effects of chemicals on employees of chemical companies through routine proximity and on the local and global community in relation to accidents and emissions;
- residues in foods due to production methods and their accumulated effects, including a consideration of the increased incidence of food allergies;
- effects of atmospheric pollution associated with fossil fuel use for heating and transportation.

iv. Social Issues

- poor employment opportunities, decline in rural services and rural community lives, for example, due to the high-tech farming methods involving larger farms with fewer workers;
- detatchment of rural sector workers from the land and fellow workers, and the implications of these for job satisfaction.

v. Visual Amenity Issues

- visual impact of monocultures, factory farms, hectares of glass; a consideration of the idea that visual pleasure is fundamentally a reward for 'what works' at a particular time;
- a consideration of the idea that landscape architects and rural planners have a role to play in creating new positive interactions between people and the environment which are at least sustainable and at best enhancing, in other words that they are potentially the architects of a new aesthetic; that plans, designs and choice of materials should be in keeping with environmental values.

The above list is not exhaustive, rather it is indicative of the size of the environmental challenge and the many links which need to be made if the full impact of rural sector activity is to be appreciated. A limited appreciation of environmental impacts begets limited environmental solutions.

In Figure 1 the various ways in which land can be used and the associated proportion of right holders is illustrated. As one moves up the triangle, value per hectare increases while the proportion of rights holders decreases. The challenge is to integrate and implement policies which pay due regard to the interests of the majority.

Figure 1 The Value Triangle

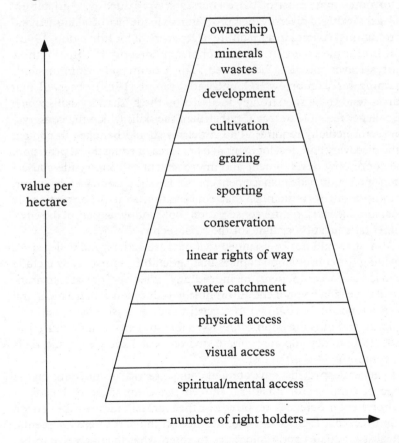

Natural Environment Research Council's Standing Committee – Land Use Research Coordinating Committee (LURCC), 'Land of Britain' (draft), 1992.

The tertiary education sector's response

The research exercise associated with this publication included the detailed scrutiny of course documentation, reference to rural sector course surveys conducted by HMI and other agencies (some of which are mentioned below) and conversations with key agencies promoting environmental responsibility within the rural sector.

The environmental connections which have been recognised by rural sector course providers relate mainly to countryside management and countryside conservation. There has been a significant growth in the provision of these courses in the last five years. The 'Environmental Responsibility' report on environmental education in the further and higher education sector notes that 'most of these courses are provided by Agricultural Colleges seeking to diversify their programmes in the face of falling demand for traditional courses in agriculture' (Department for Education, 1992).

It is also the case that the environmental integrity of some of these courses leaves much to be desired. The Countryside Commission's 'Training for Tomorrow's Countryside' report (1989) observed that courses tend to be too strongly focussed on the husbandry skills which the colleges feel able to teach, rather than the skills which the conservation sector actually requires. The criticisms should be taken in context of the discovery and development of a new area of educational provision. The continuing development and improvement of countryside conservation and countryside management courses is to be encouraged. However, it is important to remember that conservation as it is conventionally understood (that is, nature conservation) only addresses part of the environmental education agenda for the rural sector.

Also, it should not be assumed that because agricultural colleges are providing the conservation courses that agriculture courses now include a conservation component, or indeed any other appropriate environmental education component. Environmental education within agricultural colleges tends to be confined to specialist courses or specialist, optional modules, and thus the opportunity to enable students of agriculture and horticulture to develop appropriate environmental knowledge and skills and commitment is often lost.

In general, specialist environment courses service occupations on the fringe of rural sector business. Indeed the Committee of Heads of Environmental Sciences reported, in their presentation to the Toyne committee, that there is a real reluctance on the part of environmental specialist graduates and diplomates to enter, what they perceive to be, 'dirty industries'. This means that those most able to contribute to improving the environmental performance of rural sector business are not inclined to engage with the challenge.

The 'Conservation Education in Colleges of Agriculture' publication (RSPB, 1991) reported that 78 per cent of colleges in the UK did not include conservation within their mainstream courses and that few lecturers considered it their responsibility to train students in wildlife and environmental protection. The emphasis was on providing future farmers with the skills and knowledge necessary to use their land economically and efficiently to produce food.

In the same year an HMI report, 'The Response of Agricultural Colleges to Changing Needs', observed that, where it existed, 'course material relating to environmental issues was not always well organised and students did not always appreciate its significance' (Department of Education and Science, 1991).

It is important to note that agricultural colleges are not the only providers of rural environment courses. There is a proliferation of specialist routes and specialist courses relating to the rural environment for example, rural resource management, and tourism, sport and leisure courses within dedicated environment departments in the higher education sector, and particularly within the new universities. (NB: the environmental education agenda for the Catering, Tourism, Sport and Hospitality sector is considered in the Cheltenham and Gloucester College of Higher Education publication, which also belongs to the Education and Training for Business and the Environment *Taking Responsibility* series.)

Research relating to this publication reports the following trends: the ecological impact of rural sector activity is now widely acknowledged and reflected within rural sector provision. The quality of provision within some colleges is not well organised and the problem of integration into mainstream courses is still not resolved. Nevertheless, it is an area of provision which is being actively developed.

Social issues and global perspectives are routinely addressed on rural sector courses delivered by specialist environment departments, joint environment/agriculture or other rural sector specialist departments or where similar institutional or departmental partnerships have been developed, as opposed to specialist agriculture and horticulture departments or colleges where provision in these areas is at an earlier stage of development. There is also, in general, a growing emphasis on management solutions to environmental problems.

Ethical, health and visual amenity issues associated with environmental degradation caused by rural sector activity are rarely addressed within rural sector courses. The development of political literacy necessary for active citizenship and personal environmental responsibility are also rarely emphasised.

Greening vocational qualifications

Of particular future significance is the government's commitment to establish a national framework for vocational qualifications. When fully in place, the system will comprise two types of qualification: NVQs which are based on national standards of occupational competence and are intended to be delivered in the work place, and general NVQs (GNVQs) which are based on general knowledge and principles and are intended to be delivered through full-time education.

The identification, in broad terms, of NVQ environmental competences which learners need to develop is relatively easy. For example, the NVQ Level 4 in Environmental Conservation includes the following unit:

COS 21: Devise and implement environmental plans and programmes

The inclusion of environmental competences within the occupational standards is helpful. However, whilst the unit competence appears to be sound, the following associated element and performance criteria reveal real weaknesses:

Element

Gather and analyse information required to formulate plans and programmes.

Performance Criteria

- Information requirements and methods to obtain data are identified accurately and re-evaluated at suitable intervals;
- Sources of information are identified accurately and assessed for their validity, reliability, access and cost;
- Information and ideas are obtained within agreed time and cost criteria;
- Raw data are up to date, comprehensive, with agreed specification(s), and accurate to the level required;
- Where data and ideas cannot be obtained within agreed criteria, appropriate action is taken to redefine the criteria;
- Where identified information is not fully available, specific survey or information-gathering work is commissioned, recommended or carried out;
- Methods of analysis are appropriate to the type, quantity and quality of data, information and ideas available to the desired outcome;

- The analysis is cost-effective, reliable and accurate to the level required;
- Details of the analysis are recorded accurately and communicated to others where they aid decision making.

The above element refers only to plans and programmes as opposed to 'environmental' plans and programmes. It is therefore not suprising that the performance criteria relate mainly to the management of information. The ability to select the relevant information to make plans which fully take account of the environment and the environmentally sensitive analysis of this information requires an underpinning knowledge, for example, some basic concept of energy flow, natural cycles, succession, diversity, inter-relationships and so on, and the way people and societies relate to each other and natural systems. The proposition is that a basic environmental literacy is a prerequisite for environmental competency.

This link has been made within the field of environmental impact assessment. The idea of improving environmental literacy as a route to improving environmental impact assessment, and in particular improving the appraisal of data generated as a result of impact assessment, is a subject which was addressed at the 1994 International Association for Impact Assessment's (IAIA) Annual Conference on Environmental Impact Assessment in Quebec.

The report, 'Environmental Integrity of Occupational Standards' prepared by Adrian Tallis Associates for the Council for Occupational Standards and Qualifications in Environmental Conservation (1994) reviewed NVQ provision in the following areas:

- environmental conservation;

- agriculture and commercial horticulture (via ATB Landbase);

- amenity horticulture (via Amenity Horticulture Industry Lead Body);

- forestry (via Forestry and Aboriculture Lead Body);

- sport and recreation (via Sport and Recreation Lead Body);

- waste management (via Waste Management Industry Training and Advisory Board).

The report recommended a rationalisation of methods including environmental references within occupational qualifications in the above areas of provision, and the adoption of a wider view of environmental issues through standards, with particular reference to resource management and recycling.

In summary, the difficulties associated with 'greening' NVQs relate to insufficient and inconsistent references to the environment in competence statements and performance criteria; limited opportunities for contextual teaching, because of the amount of time required for the teaching and assessment of the prescribed skills; and the generally low level of environmental literacy of teaching staff.

GNVQs offer a more favourable setting for the development of environmental literacy and competency. There are various routes through which these developments can be facilitated including:

• stand-alone environment GNVQ;

• mandatory units;

• optional units;

• additional units;

• integration within existing units.

The University of Hertfordshire's Environmental Responsibility Centre has been commissioned to research these options and make recommendations to the National Council for Vocational Qualifications (NCVQ).

There has been some experimentation with the development of a GNVQ for land-based industries. Current opinion seems to favour a GNVQ which covers general environmental principles. Such a development, for example at levels two and three, would provide appropriate underpinning of environmental knowledge and skills for land-based industries, for example farming, and a whole range of other occupations, for example small businesses. An environment GNVQ level four could be the equivalent of the common core of environmental specialist courses.

Consensus seems to be developing around a generic environmental education agenda which is relevant to all students. References to this common agenda have appeared in the following:

• Toyne Report (2.4 and 6.37);

• BTEC's Environmental Initiative publication;

- IES (Institution of Environmental Sciences) position paper;

- Cross-curricular Environmental Education Framework paper, endorsed by Professor Toyne and the Committee of Heads of Environmental Sciences;

- COSQUEC's draft proposal for Common Standards of Competence in relation to environmental management.

1.3   Trends Towards Curriculum 'Greening'

Enabling policies and initiatives
There are a number of policies and initiatives which both endorse the need for, and encourage, the greening of the FHE curriculum, and which, in turn, create a pressure for a whole institution response to environmental concerns.

Agenda 21: Agenda 21 is a key outcome of the United Nations Conference on Environment and Development, popularly known as the Earth Summit, held in Rio De Janeiro in June 1992. Agenda 21 is a comprehensive, forward-looking action plan to guide sustainable development. Chapter 36 paragraph 5 (b) states: 'Governments should strive to update or prepare strategies aimed at integrating environment and development as a cross-cutting issue into education at all levels within the next three years ...' (that is, 1992–1995).

A Commission for Sustainable Development (CSD) has been set up, under the aegis of the UN, to monitor progress in implementing the agreements reached in Rio, actions being taken to implement Agenda 21.

European Community Policy: The European Community resolution passed in May 1988 (88/C 177/03) requires that each member state should 'promote environmental education in all sectors', the objective being 'to lay the foundations for a fully informed and active participation of the individual in the protection of the environment and the prudent and rational use of national resources.' The Community's Fifth Environmental Action Programme (1992) calls for the 'speeding up of substantive imple-mentation of the Resolution.' It also identifies five sectors for particular attention – agriculture, industry, energy, transport and tourism – in recog-nition of their significant and damaging environmental impact.

UK Government Policies and Initiatives: The government White Paper on the Environment ('This Common Inheritance', September 1990) emphasises the need for all citizens to play their part towards the achievement of sustainability. Although the government's approach to further and higher education is that course providers should be free of unnecessary controls, it is exerting some pressure on institutions to assist in producing environmentally responsible, active citizens.

The White Paper on the Environment states that: 'It is important that environmental concerns are reflected in science, engineering and other courses in further and higher education' (17.48).

The Department for Education set up an expert committee in October 1991 to look at environmental education in the context of the needs of industry. This initiative stemmed from the government White Paper on the Environment, section 17.49. The committee's report, 'Environmental Responsibility: An Agenda for Further and Higher Education' was published in February 1993. It lays considerable emphasis on 'cross-curricular greening' which it describes as 'poorly developed'. Key points include:

- FHE has an important role to play in developing the environmental understanding of students whose courses are not specifically 'environmental' in focus;

- such 'cross-curricular greening' may be concerned with work-related needs, or more broadly with the students' needs as citizens. In practice, much provision may address both sets of needs concurrently;

- although many employers see a need for 'greening', it has not so far received the attention it deserves either from FHE institutions or from national examining validating and accrediting bodies.

Recommendations relating to cross-curricular greening include:

- each institution, pursuant to its overall environmental policy, should adopt a policy for the development of environmental education;

- insofar as future funding arrangements for FHE involve earmarked provision for staff development in particular subject areas, serious consideration should be given by the further and higher education funding councils to the claims of environmental education.

Sustainable Development: the UK Strategy: In January 1994 the UK government launched four strategy documents produced in response to commitments made at the Earth Summit 1992. These were: Sustainable Development: the UK Strategy; Biodiversity: the UK action plan; Sustainable Forestry: the UK programme; and Climate Change: the UK programme.

Sustainable Development: the UK Strategy document states:

> Education and training are crucial to the achievement of sustainable development. They can provide the population, including the workforce, with an understanding of how the environment relates to everyday issues and what action they can take personally to reduce their own impact on the environment at home, at work and in their leisure activities (Paragraph 32.12, p. 209).

It also reported that: 'The government is investigating the feasibility of establishing an Environmental Standards Forum whose objectives would include providing assistance on the "greening of standards" and helping with the future development of GNVQs' (Paragraph 33.30, p. 17).

Education and Training for Business and the Environment Programme: see preface.

The National Curriculum: Environmental education is one of the National Curriculum's five cross-curricular themes. The National Curriculum also includes a solid statutory foundation for environmental education, extending to sustainable development, in geography and science. The benefits of this have been reduced somewhat in the light of the decision to make geography discretionary post-14 years (cf the Dearing Report, 1994).

The National Curriculum requires students to develop knowledge and understanding of:

- the natural processes which take place in the environment;

- the impact of human activities on the environment;

- different environments, both past and present;

- environmental issues such as the greenhouse effect, acid rain, air pollution;

- local, national and international legislative controls to protect and manage the environment

- how policies and decisions are made about the environment;

- the environmental interdependence of individuals, groups, communities and nations;

- how human lives and livelihoods are dependent on the environment;

- the conflicts which can arise around environmental issues;

- how the environment has been affected by past decisions and actions;

- the importance of planning, design and aesthetic considerations;

- the importance of effective action to protect and manage the environment.

This can be used as a framework for questioning new students about their environmental knowledge and understanding and a check-list of themes for development.

Whatever foundations have been made in schools, there is a need to build on them. To promote environmental education at a school level and not at the further and higher education level conveys the unfortunate message that concern for the environment has nothing to do with the world of work.

Business and Technology Education Council (BTEC): The aim of this initiative is to offer guidance to teachers of BTEC courses on the application of environmental learning outcomes, in order to enable students to make personal and future work-related decisions which take account of the environment. To this end BTEC has developed, at national level, a series of environmental learning outcomes relating to: environmental responsibility; science and technology; resource management; business practice; policy and control; and investigation.

Lead bodies
There are three lead bodies which are substantially concerned with improving the environmental competence of the workforce in their sectors. The first is the Council for Occupational Standards and Qualifications

in Environmental Conservation. This body is developing National Vocational Qualifications and Scottish Vocational qualifications (SNVQs) for archaeology, landscapes and ecosystems (including landscape and countryside conservation, countryside recreation and environmental interpretation), building conservation and sustainable resource management (including pollution control, recycling and waste management).

The second lead body is the Waste Management Industry Training Advisory Board (WAMITAB) and the third, the Board for Education and Training in the Water Industry (BETWI).

It is important to note that COSQUEC's remit extends beyond producing standards and qualifications within its own sphere of interest to influencing and promoting standards in other relevant occupational sectors.

Industry's view

There still persists a lack of understanding on the part of industry with regards to what environmental specialists have to offer. There also persists a reluctance on the part of environmental specialists to enter industry. The preconceptions of industry and environmental specialists are complicating the debate surrounding specialist provision.

However, industry is clear about the need for the 'cross-curricular greening' of the further and higher education curricula. The following quotations are indicative of this: 'industry's need is for an environmentally literate workforce rather that environmental specialists' (The CBI's response to the Toyne committee's industry survey, 1992);

'Respondents believed that some degree of environmental awareness should be incorporated into training and education at all levels and in all disciplines to provide a basic appreciation of good environmental husbandry and what this involved' (Towards Environmental Competence in Scotland: Phase 2: Industry in Commerce, Scottish Enterprise, 1991)

The greening of the FHE curriculum may be the only way of introducing environmental thinking into the practices of small and medium sized companies, who are largely unaware that they have any environmental responsibilities and are therefore unlikely to consider environmentally educating their existing staff. Large environmentally proactive companies are beginning to address the staff development issue.

Students' view

Students are very concerned about the environment. There are examples of students initiating action at a strategic level within their colleges. The recurring message from consumer surveys, the National Union of Students and student unions in general is that students are increasingly likely to choose to study at educational institutions which take their environmental responsibilities seriously.

The main source of information about a college's environmental position is through its prospectus. At best this highlights the college's environmental policy and specialist courses. At the moment there is no information about the actual environmental performance of educational institutions, and as such students are currently unable to make informed choices.

Public perception

Public perception of what constitutes good practice is of key importance. There is no doubt that local authorities, waste contractors, and local rural businesses are increasingly aware of the need to have good relations with their local communities. For instance, local waste contractors may decide not to landfill loads of paper or dust-generating waste (even though it may be legally allowed) because they know that it would blow around the neighbourhood and cause complaints. In other words, the voice of the public is listened to.

The educational challenge is to improve public perception of the environmental impacts which are most damaging to them. Because cause and effect are often separated in space and time the public is largely unaware of the environmentally damaging nature of a whole range of local activities and thus unable to express appropriate concern.

2 THE ENVIRONMENTAL EDUCATION AGENDA FOR RURAL SECTOR COURSE PROVIDERS

2.1 Institutional Development

Students can learn useful environmental lessons from institutions which are sustainably managed. The disadvantage is that the learning environment communicates powerful messages, whether it is sustainably managed or not. As such, students at institutions where resources are not used wisely can learn not to value the environment. This can result in environmentally insensitive behaviour and the negation of environmental education delivered through course curricula.

The environmental contextualisation of further and higher education curricula must therefore be set in the context of a wider strategy, akin to the corporate environmental strategies which an increasing number of companies are adopting.

Compared with a chemical plant, the environmental impact of an academic institution is modest. Nevertheless, a typical institution, among other things:

- has a multi-million pound turnover;

- has the ownership or use of a good deal of more or less well cared-for real estate;

- is a substantial and more or less wasteful user of energy, water, paper and many other materials (by no means all of them 'eco-friendly', and some of them positively hazardous);

- operates a large-scale catering facility which is likely to generate substantial waste;

- is visited every day by large numbers of people, using various modes of transport.

The Toyne Report recommends that every FHE institution should formally adopt and publicise, by the beginning of the academic year 1994/5, a comprehensive environmental policy statement together with an action plan for its implementation. Policy development is of key importance. It begins the process of accountability which ties in the participation of all institution members and provides encouragement and permission for individual initiatives.

For details of the scope of an institutional response to the environment please see *Colleges Going Green: A Guide to Environmental Action in Further Education Colleges* (Ali Khan, 1992).

Capel Manor's Environmental Policy

Policy Aim

To encourage and develop all staff at Capel Manor Environmental and Horticultural Centre to increase their understanding of the environment and how their actions may affect it. To enable them to make informed assessment of their working practices, and to act in a way which, if possible, will reduce or eliminate any negative environmental impacts.

Policy Objectives

These may be broken down into three main areas:

i. Staff

- to create an environmental ethic among all the staff so that in all their working activities they consider the environmental consequences;
- to encourage staff to work together in teams to identify and improve environmental impacts which concern, affect and can be affected by their team;
- to provide each area of work of Capel Manor with a training focus at which environmental knowledge can be shared by each team.

ii. Resources

- to examine all the resources which are used in every section at Capel Manor and identify their environmental impact; to investigate environmentally friendly alternatives and study the possibilities of using them or not using the resource at all;
- to examine proposed new developments and new purchases and assess them against sound environmental criteria;
- to enquire of suppliers the detailed environmental qualities of their products and procedures.

iii. Procedures

- to review all procedures used at Capel Manor and identify those which are inefficient or wasteful, and adopt a corrective strategy;

- to identify services to clients, customers and visitors and ensure they are environmentally sound;
- to monitor and assess continually environmental improvements and changes, and direct financial gains to other environmental improvements;
- to publicise the sound environmental actions that are taken, which may encourage others to do likewise.

Education institutions which specialise in rural sector courses traditionally use their farms and estates as educational resources. These institutions are particularly likely to receive criticism from students and lecturers if environmental principles delivered through the curriculum are not matched in practice. College farms and estates are also visited by local schools and more generally by the local community, for both learning and leisure. These groups also have expectations of good environmental practice, however they perceive it.

The benefits of opening up the walls of our classrooms, 'those anaesthetising barriers of comfort and avoidance' (O'Riordan, 1993) are now well documented. O'Riordan moves the debate on a little further by suggesting that:

> the classrooms of the future should be the culmination of local initiatives of the sustainable transition. These are the laboratories of both learning and training where the Agenda 21 'stakeholder groups' – industry, women, youth, farmers, trades unions, scientists and environmental organisations – can work with local governments and those relevant indigenous peoples to outreach to a common cause.

The following case study is an example of a local initiative of the sustainable transition and thus must qualify as an example of 'a classroom of the future'.

Stanaway 'LEAF' Farm, Otley College, Suffolk

Positioned on the edge of the village of Otley, six miles north of Ipswich, Suffolk, Stanaway Farm is typical of the heavy land farms in the area. As host to Otley College of Agriculture which leases 22 hectares of the farm, it performs an educational role. This role stems from the aims of Stanaway Farm's owner since 1966, the Felix Cobbold Agricultural Trust, a charity formed in 1909 to promote agricultural education and good farming practices.

Stanaway Farm has been selected to participate in the Linking Environment and Farming (LEAF) project, which is based at the National

Agricultural Centre, Warwickshire. The aim of the project is to develop and promote systems of agriculture which meet economic, environmental and agronomic objectives.

A key concept is Integrated Crop Management which is a combination of responsible farming practices which balance the economic production of crops, through the appropriate rotations and cultivations, careful choice of seed variety, judicious use of crop production inputs and conservation measures. A key emphasis is on the production of safe, wholesome food.

A prerequisite for participation in the LEAF project is a commitment to practise and promote a whole-farm management approach. LEAF has produced guidance for environmental auditing to assist farmers to:

• look objectively at their business and assess strengths and weaknesses;

• target resources;

• monitor progress;

• compare operations;

• identify cost saving operations;

• reassure authorities that legislation is being followed and that health and safety measures are being carried out;

• raise employee awareness of environmental issues;

• ensure key issues are focussed upon, for example training;

• gain credit for good environmental performance.

The LEAF environmental audit addresses eight principal areas:

• landscape features;

• wildlife and habitats;

• soil management;

• crop protection;

- conservation of energy;

- pollution control;

- organisation and planning;

- animal welfare.

LEAF farmers are required to comply with relevant legislation and government codes of practice, and are encouraged to make use of appropriate advisory services, for example, the Farming and Wildlife Advisory Group.

2.2   Curriculum Development for Rural Course Providers

The Education and Training for Business and the Environment *Taking Responsibility* series, to which this publication belongs, is aimed at the higher education sector. However, much of the education for the rural sector is delivered by the further education sector. Within this section there are case studies from both sectors to encourage the cross-fertilisation of ideas.

Case studies have been selected to illustrate details of content relating to areas of environmental education provision which are poorly developed, and to stimulate thinking in relation to pedagogy. There can be no attempt within this brief publication to represent a comprehensive account of the good environmental education practice which exists across rural sector course provision.

Strategic developments
One outcome of the Education for Business and the Environment seminar and research project on environmental education across higher education curricula has been the identification of what I have called a Framework for Cross-Curricular Environmental Education relevant to all students which is the first case study in this section. A little more specific is the second case study, the BTEC learning outcome set, relating to resource management. The final case is the Netherlands check-list of questions and a suggested process to encourage the routine consideration of the environmental implications of agriculture sector practice.

Framework for Cross-Curricular Environmental Education

The following environmental education framework relating to cross-curricular provision, developed by the author, has been endorsed by Peter Toyne, the chair of the Department for Education's expert committee on environmental education in further and higher education; the Committee of Heads of Environmental Sciences; and the Institution of Environmental Sciences. The overall objective of the framework is to enable further and higher education students to develop the ability and commitment to manage their personal and work-related environmental responsibilities.

The framework is described in terms of learning outcomes which are a useful device for describing 'ends' which are linked to educational purposes, without prescribing means, and thus avoiding telling lecturers what and how to teach. The content associated with the learning outcomes is indicative rather than prescriptive.

The framework may be regarded as an agenda for personal engagement with the environmental problems of today, as well as a collective search for a deeper understanding of our environmental connections. It is designed to encourage positive involvement and enhancement as opposed to damage limitation.

The framework states that every student leaving the further and higher education should be able to:

i.   Understand the principles of sustainability: these relate to biodiversity; environmental values and ethics; natural cycles; people as part of nature; quality of human life (as opposed to standard of living); the depletion of finite resources; and the earth's carrying capacity.

ii. Recognise the environmental impact of personal choices and decisions and potential contribution to environmental solutions: these relate to choice and/or use of: cleaning materials; clothes; energy; food; hobbies; holidays; household durables; transport; water.

iii. Recognise the environmental impact of chosen educational/occupational areas and their potential contribution to environmental solutions: whilst this learning outcome is relevant to all students, the environmental impacts and contributions will vary according to student specialism.

iv. Appreciate the relationships between human activity and global environmental problems such as: acid rain; desertification; ozone depletion; global warming; toxic waste.

v. Appreciate the contribution and limitation of current approaches to environmental solutions: these include economic; legislative; managerial (for example BS7750); media-led campaigns; scientific; and technological approaches.

vi. Manage personal and work-related environmental responsibilities: the successful achievement of this learning outcome will depend on the development of: appropriate awareness and understanding (see learning outcomes i–v), a sense of environmental responsibility, and associated skills. This would enable students to:

- conduct interdisciplinary analysis/appraisal which might include the use of techniques such as environmental impact assessment, life-cycle analysis and environmental auditing;
- make critical judgments;
- manage change;
- manage information;
- participate in organisational politics;
- think creatively.

BTEC Learning Outcome Series: Resource Management

In the context of the learners area of resource management and present or future responsibility, he/she should be able to:

i. appreciate the characteristics of the resource/s to be managed and its/their value to people;

ii. appreciate the environmental implications of the uncontrolled use of the resources to be managed;

iii. recognise when the use of a resource needs to be stopped or limited, or when it requires protection;

iv. propose alternative ways of meeting the human wants and needs met by resources which are being over-exploited or degraded;

v. make resource management decisions which take account of the environment.

NB: These learning outcomes apply equally to natural and physical resources and are relevant to all learners whose future work has resource responsibilities. Examples of performance criteria and range are included in the BTEC Environmental Initiative publication (Ali Khan, 1992).

Integration of Environmental Aspects into Agricultural Education in the Netherlands

The Integration of Environmental Aspects in Agricultural Education (IMAO) project was initiated by the Directorate of Agricultural Education in the Ministry of Agriculture, Nature Conservation and Fisheries (Netherlands) in 1988. The project was executed by the Institute for the Development of Agricultural Pedagogy and Schooling (STOAS). Since 1992 this project has formed part of the so-called Long-term Plan for Education in Nature and Environment.

One outcome of the above project has been the development of an environmental awareness-raising check-list, a tool to enable teachers and course developers to give environmental concerns concrete expression in teaching. The check-list is essentially a series of steps which teachers and learners are encouraged to work through as a matter of routine, to encourage environmental responsibility. The IMAO Checklist is arranged as follows:

Taking Stock
Answer the following questions:

1. Which environmental aspects are relevant to the action?
2. What are the possible environmental effects of the action?
3. How does the environmental effect of the action originate or operate?
4. On what part of the environment has the action a direct effect?
5. On what part of the environment has the action an indirect effect?
6. Where does the environmental impact of the action occur?
7. When does the environmental impact of the action occur?
8. What is the extent or significance of the environmental effect of the action?
8. For what reasons is the action carried out in an environmentally harmful way?
9. What reasons are there for acting in alternative ways which cause less environmental damage?

Alternatives
Describe the relevant and available environment-friendly alternative actions in terms of knowledge and skills by repeating questions 1-8.

Compare the advantages and disadvantages of the various alternative actions.

Choice
Make a sound choice.

Realisation
Carry out the action with environmental awareness.

Evaluation
Review and assess critically alternative actions regularly; be alert to changing views and information on the environmental effects of alternative actions.

Institutional developments
The emphasis in this publication, and more generally in the Promoting Sustainable Practice through Higher Education Curricula series is on the integration of appropriate environmental education components into existing course provision as opposed to specialist environmental provision. However, the distinction between the two is not as clear as it might at first appear, especially where there are significant environmental links with subject areas. For instance, is a course in rural resource management a specialist environment course or a specialist rural sector course set in its appropriate environmental context?

Both generic and specialist elements of specialist environment provision have cross-curricular relevance. The integration of specialist provision into existing tertiary curricula would facilitate the greening process. Unfortunately, specialist environment schools and departments have no brief to play a strategic role in greening their institution's curricula.

The first case study in this section, Seale Hayne's Rural Policy Analysis Unit, was chosen to illustrate how socioeconomic considerations can be brought together with natural world concerns and how political literacy can be fostered.

The second case study, Worcester College's Permaculture course, has been featured to illustrate the need for institutions to engage in the search for solutions.

The third, the University of Edinburgh's Institute of Ecology and Resource Management policy statement, is an example of how general environmental education principles can be made explicit for a wide range of courses. The themes outlined in the Institute's specialist course on Applied Animal Behaviour and Animal Welfare have relevance for all students who are likely to have responsibility for animals in their future work.

The fourth study, the Anglia University/Writtle College Rural Resource Development degree, illustrates the importance of partnerships in developing interdisciplinary courses and the concept of a common interdisciplinary core as the basis for specialist environment courses, as recommended in the Toyne Report (4.15). This common core also has cross-curricular relevance.

The fifth case study, Reading University's BSc in Rural Resource Mangement, is illustrative of the recent emergence of number of courses of this title.

The sixth and final case study, Wye College's MSc in Environmental Management, is illustrative of two trends: the proliferation of specialist environmental MSc courses, and a recognition of the role of environmental management in the pursuit of environmental solutions. The course outline makes reference to the touchstones of environmental education which apply to both specialist and cross-curricular provision, namely: acknowledgement of an underlying environmental ethic; encouragement of holistic thinking; progressive stance; and promotion of an interdisciplinary perspective.

Seale Hayne, University of Plymouth: BSc Rural Estate Management, Rural Policy Analysis Unit

The rationale behind this 50-hour course is that rural societies and rural businesses exist within an environment influenced by government policy, together with other socioeconomic forces. As such, the student must be able to analyse and evaluate this policy within its socioeconomic context and in the light of relevant theories of decision-making, in order to understand how and why it exists and has developed, and might change in the future.

The course aims to explore relevant aspects of government policy in order to explain what has happened, predict what might happen, and assess the advantages and limitations of different policy options.

The principal objectives (and content) consists of the following challenges:

i.   Explain the operation of a free market in agricultural products, identifying its special characteristics: analysis of agricultural product and rural resource markets; agricultural price instability; implications of the long-term decline of free market constant farm prices; the structure of the agricultural industry; the reasons for and implications of instability in international trade in agricultural products.

ii. Explain how and why, and with what results, governments make decisions on agricultural policy and predict the decisions that might be made in the future: objectives and methods of intervention in agriculture by governments and intergovernmental organisations; the development of agricultural policy in the UK and the EC; the Common Agricultural Policy (CAP); an assessment of the explanatory and predictive capacity of various economic and political models of decision-making in the EC; evaluation of the CAP; the interaction of agricultural and other rural policies.

iii. Review the economics of the forestry industry and assess the costs and benefits of current forestry policy: analysis of the market for forest products; comparison of discounted cash flow and discounted consumption flow methods; the structure of the forest industry; international trade in forest industry; international trade in forest products; economic and non-economic objectives in forest policy; evaluation of forestry policy.

iv. Explain why pollution occurs, assess optimum control levels, and compare the economic implications of alternative control methods: the concept of externalities; assessment and comparison of social costs and benefits; economic and political advantages and limitations of alternative control methods.

v. Explain the special problems which arise in the economic analysis of natural resources and assess the implications of various resource exploitation strategies: the classical economics of natural resource use; classification of natural resources; behaviour of markets for different categories of natural resource; natural resource policy.

Worcester College of Agriculture: Permaculture courses

The word 'Permaculture' was coined by an Australian, Bill Mollinson, to describe a radical approach to agricultural design. It is the conscious use of ecological principles in designing self-sustaining food, fibre and energy producing ecosystems. The idea is to set up systems for human use which emphasise the use of diversity (of species and activities), interdependence, recycling, conservation and stability.

Permaculture is about design, not technique. Within it many techniques can be used – organic growing and pest control techniques; forest farming and old forestry practices such as coppicing; free-range poultry and animal raising; technology for energy conservation and the use of solar energy; and recycling of wastes. The key issue is the way all the different elements are consciously designed to work together creating an intricate web of interrelationships which is both stable and high-yielding.

Permaculture offers a set of design principles. It is up to the user to apply these principles with intelligence and knowledge to suit a particular circumstance. There are no rules, and the underlying philosophy is to encourage the use of common sense and local knowledge. This can be likened to rediscovering and developing on a conscious and informed level the wisdom of ancient polycultures which continued for centuries in balance with their surroundings.

The college offers a number of courses about permaculture, and the internationally recognised design course is available as a block or as an evening course. Courses in relation to the application of permaculture principles to forest garden design and gardening are also offered.

University of Edinburgh, Institute of Ecology and Resource Management: Educational Policy and Post Graduate Diploma in Applied Animal Behaviour and Animal Welfare

The policy aims of the institute are to:

•   understand the fundamental process of biology, the environment and economics, and to apply this understanding to the sustainable management of the world's biological resources;

•   develop an interdisciplinary approach to agriculture, ecology, forestry and economics and so build a holistic view of land, water, air and plant and animal management;

•   employ quantitative and qualitative approaches to assist the understanding of the relationship between humankind and the environment.

Post Graduate MSc/Diploma course in Applied Animal Behaviour And Animal Welfare

The objective of this one year course is to provide a knowledge of animal behaviour which can be fruitfully applied in science and practice. Especially, the course will allow an objective assessment of the welfare of animals in farmed, maintained and wild conditions. The course is suitable for qualified agronomists, veterinarians and biologists who will have to make assessments of help, prepare legislation on animal welfare, or carry out research into the subjects of animal behaviour, welfare and protection.

The academic content of the course includes: social behaviour; the neural basis of behaviour; the basis of pain distress and discomfort; motivation; behavioural problems in companion animals; statistics; computing; human–animal interactions; wildlife management; pest control by behavioural means; applied animal behaviour; cognition in animals; the assessment of welfare; the design of relevant investigations; philosophy and animal welfare; legislation and animal welfare; improvement of welfare; alternative systems of animal production and maintenance; animal protection.

Anglia University in Partnership with Writtle Agricultural College:
BSc Hons in Rural Resource Management

This course developed from a recognition by staff at both centres that their education programmes were ignoring the interrelationships between the competing demands on the countryside. They considered their courses to be producing graduates whose attitudes were leading to problems in rural areas. Academic staff with agricultural, leisure, development, conservation and planning backgrounds were brought together to develop the new course.

The team also consulted over 70 countryside-based public and private organisations who pointed out the need for targeted routes relating to specific professions and occupations. The outcome of the consultation process was the development of an interdisciplinary core which includes science, business, law and socioeconomic modules, and a range of specialist options. The course also has an industrial advisory panel. It is very popular, and attracts in the order of 70 students per year, all of whom are required to carry out a work-shadowing exercise for three weeks within a rural agency.

The aims of the course have much in common with the BTEC learning outcomes relating to resource management.

Reading University: BSc in Rural Resource Management

The Rural Resource Management degree is offered jointly by the Department of Agriculture and the Department of Agricultural Economics and Management.

The following questions are addressed by this course:

- how can farmers adapt to the changing requirements of the market-place and government policy?

- is modern food production compatible with the maintenance of an attractive landscape and the conservation of woodland, marshes and other wildlife habitats?

- how can we value the environment?

- should the transformation of farmland into housing developments, golf courses, theme parks and community forests be encouraged or restricted?

- as farm employment falls, how can alternative rural employment opportunities be developed?

- should there be greater access to the countryside, and at what cost?

Students are encouraged to take a balanced view of rural sector issues and to develop a range of problem-solving skills. The nature of rural resources and the activities based upon them form a basis for exploring environmental impacts and competing interests, policy options and the role of government. The course features a wide range of visits and practical projects.

Wye College, University of London: MSc in Environmental Management; Distance Learning Package

Students have to complete successfully seven courses, four in Part I and three in Part II. Part I consists of concepts of the environment in the social sciences; economics for environmental management; environmental science; and principles and methods in environmental management.

Concepts of the environment in the social sciences: this course examines the way the environment is understood in different cultures, and the assumptions that underlie the way the environment is managed. Three distinctive approaches are assessed: political economy, technical 'managerialism' and deep ecology. Exploring the concept of sustainable development, the course investigates the way that the countryside and 'wilderness' are understood in different societies.

Economics for environmental management: this is divided into three sections. The first examines the concepts and principles, including the market model in environmental management, economic growth versus sustainable development, and international issues such as debt-for-nature swaps. The second section deals with economic instruments and their application to pollution control, the management of renewable resources and the depletion of exhaustible resources. Finally, there is a discussion of public decision-making and the use of such techniques as cost-benefit analysis.

Environmental science: this course aims to demonstrate that the earth, atmosphere and water systems form a coherent and interactive whole. The first part deals with the atmosphere and hydrosphere and includes discussion of world climates and the management of water resources. The second part is concerned with the earth and the use of its minerals and soils. The third part examines the major factors affecting the distribution and abundance of plants and animals, and relates them to environmental management. Finally, under 'managing for survival', topics include global warming, energy alternatives, the loss of biological diversity and waste recycling.

Principles and methods in environmental management: this provides an essential opportunity to reflect upon the underlying ethics and choices that inform environmental management practices. It takes issues and explores different cultural, political and social dimensions, illustrating the essentially interdisciplinary character of environmental management. The course will examine the practice of environmental management in different regions ranging from arid lands to tropical forests and from temperate river systems to arctic coasts. The course will apply methods in meteorology, hydrology, geomorphology, ecology, and the measurement of air and water quality.

Part II consists of three courses chosen from a number of options, subject to availability. These options are: environmental impact assessment; environmental valuation: theory, techniques and applications; water resources management; environmental values and ethics; sustainable agricultural development; and international environmental law and policy.

It is possible to substitute for one of the Part II courses a dissertation or piece of original research based on the student's work experience.

Sample learning activities
Enabling students to be active environmental citizens includes the development of personal transferable skills. This has implications for pedagogy.

The 'deep' approach to learning seems to be compatible with the development of active citizenship skills. This approach emphasises independence of mind and the ability to make sense of rather than reproduce information. According to Graham Gibb (1992) 'Deep' learning approaches include:

- independent learning;

- personal development;

- problem based learning;

- reflection;

- independent group work;

- learning by doing;

- developing learning skills;

- project work.

The following four case studies are in keeping with the 'deep' approach to learning.

BTEC National Level Module: Agriculture in a World Context: Assignment; developed by the Farmers World Network

In this module learners investigate the production and international trade of sugar and suggest ways forward for the sugar industry in the context of sustainable agricultural production worldwide. Learners work in small groups and investigate one of the following situations per group: the production of sugar in the Philippines from sugar cane; the production of sugar substitutes from maize in the USA, that is High Fructose Corn Syrup (HFCS); or the production of sugar in Europe.

Each of the groups is asked to consider the following factors in their investigation:

- the impact of the production process on the environment and on the local social structure;

- how the present situation developed;

- the technology used in the production process; and

- the international trade situation.

Each group is required to prepare a poster display for use in an exhibition including, where appropriate, newspaper cuttings, leaflets, photographs, and a short group presentation to peers followed by a debate on the difference and interactions between the three situations. An individual report suggesting ways forward for the sugar industry worldwide is also part of the assessment.

First Year BSc Hons in Environmental Studies; major study element: Reconstruction of a Public Inquiry, Developed by Manchester Metropolitan University

The overall aim of this programme is to acquaint students with the conflicts facing decision-makers, to familiarise them with the function of local and national authorities in the environmental decision-making process and to encourage objective thought. Students participate as the public when asking questions at the inquiry and are asked to prepare their own inspector's report to the secretary of state as the linked assignment.

The exercise centres on an authentic appeal against a quarry extension planning application previously refused by the local authority. The proposed site, near Castleton in the Peak District National Park, contains a Site of Special Scientific Interest (SSSI) and is popular with cavers and tourists. However, the appellants (a mining company) are pointing to a high demand for limestone in the vicinity which could only be fulfilled by existing quarry extension or by quarrying elsewhere. The company argues that the former would be more economic and cause less disturbance. The appeal is to be considered by an inspector from the Department of the Environment.

In the introductory programme the students are given a series of lectures and seminars which outline the background to the appeal and the structure of the decision-making process in planning applications. In addition they are taken on a site inspection to see the quarry and surrounding areas. Finally they attend the inquiry itself.

The case is re-enacted before a group of about 100 students. Representatives for the appellants include the QC, who presents the case, and witnesses, including a landscape manager, a minerals consultant and the quarry manager. Permission was denied previously by the Peak Park Joint Planning Board who are supported by an ecologist, a speleologist and representatives from the Countryside Commission, the Council for the Protection of Rural England, English Nature and the Ramblers Association.

Conflicts in the evidence, the ambiguous nature of the 60 pages of information presented and the live delivery give scope for students to participate and to attempt to develop a balanced recommendation to the secretary of state.

The learning exercise is designed to develop:

• an appreciation of the conflict between legitimate commercial/economic and environmental considerations in rural situations;

• an understanding of bias and variation in modes of written and oral presentation of evidence;

• an appreciation of the difficulties of making objective decisions and recommendations in real-world situations;

• report writing skills.

Diploma in Agriculture: assignment on Pollution Management Control, developed by Newton Rigg College

The assignment links directly to processes put in place on the college farms in conjunction with the National Rivers Authority. Preparation for the assignment includes: viewing NRA film on water quality; farm walk round lowland farm Newton Rigg; a discussion on the principles of the Newton Rigg farm's pollution control plan; and a visit to Low Beckside hill farm accompanied by NRA representative. The aim of the assignment is to assess the quantity of slurry produced at Low Beckside farm, and to suggest its safe storage and disposal.

Students are provided with: Low Beckside farm maps, building plans, stock numbers, and the Newton Rigg farm Pollution Management Plan. They are required to:

• calculate the amount of slurry produced in a typical winter;

• calculate the total nitrogen spread in the form of slurry;

• produce a Pollution Management Control plan for Low Beckside;

• calculate the amount of bagged fertiliser required to meet the requirements of the stock;

- discuss their findings with their tutor.

They have access to the following information sources: Code of Good Agricultural Practice for the Protection of Water – MAFF; the Influence of Agriculture on the Quality of Natural Waters in England and Wales – NRA; Cement and Concrete Association guides; Scottish Colleges monthly reports.

The completed assignments are jointly assessed by the college and the NRA. All students are required to discuss their findings with the assessors.

Department of Environmental and Biological Sciences: fieldwork for the environment, developed by Liverpool Institute of Higher Education (LIHE)

Environmental education has been defined in terms of the trilogy: about the environment, in the environment and for the environment. However, there is a reluctance shared by both academics and students within higher education institutions to engage in action for the environment. This is associated with a perception that action for the environment is beneath loftier, conceptual and theoretical pursuits. The introduction of action for the environment into the LIHE's Department of Environmental and Biological Sciences was the result of one person's initiative. It is now a tradition within the department.

For example, the LIHE has established contacts with the Snowdonia National Park Study Centre. Over several years, students have been involved in a wide range of activities. One of the most memorable was the excavation and drainage of (a very small) part of the medieval droving road between Harlech and Dolgellau from 30cm of peat and silt. This was carried out in conjunction with the British Trust for Conservation Volunteers.

For such projects appropriate clothing and equipment is essential, and students must be aware of the hazards associated with each task, the environment in which they work and the tools they use: Staff must be similarly aware and also have appropriate safety equipment on site and all activities should be set within a conceptual and theoretical framework; they should be small, tangible, and able to be completed in the available time. In addition activities should be assessed.

The benefits of such fieldwork are numerous. In the first instance students are given an opportunity for exertion, which most find a pleasant change. This is combined with the fact that they also have an opportunity to do something positive for the environment, which makes them feel good, as well as providing them with an understanding of the purposeful nature of environmental education. Contact with adults and organisations from the working world is interesting and potentially useful in their future careers, and they learn to appreciate the role of management in the execution of group tasks. Finally it is also an opportunity to put theory into practice.

BSc Landscape Management and Rural Resource Management, Forestry and Woodlands module: Project to develop an Urban Woodland Plan, developed by Reading University

The task of this project is to produce an Urban Woodland Plan for an area adjoining Clayfield copse in Caversham. The project is in two parts. First, each group should produce a written report of between 2500 and 3000 words describing its plan for the area. The report contributes 75 per cent towards individual project marks and includes an element of peer assessment. The remaining 25 per cent will be awarded for Part 2, which requires that each group produce a visual display of its plan. Groups will be questioned about their displays during the assessment. The display judged to be the best will be featured in the foyer of the Civic Offices as part of the Reading Borough Council's exhibition for National Tree Week.

The council brief on which the students base their work consists of the following:

The Borough Council has decided to redevelop an area of land on the margins of Caversham. The area is owned by the Council, though the arable land is currently rented out to a farmer. This arable land is to be brought back into public use, to complement the adjoining recreational areas. We would like to produce an urban woodland development plan for this area, based on the following brief.

The two woodland sites already existing are Clayfield copse itself, designated as a local nature reserve under the 1949 National Parks and Access to the Countryside Act, and Blackhouse Woods, the south-western two-thirds of which are owned by Reading Borough Council. These two woodlands are ecologically very important, especially in the local context. Any tree planting in the area should not affect this, and should be composed of non-competitive species, or some form of buffer zone.

There are two hedgerows, both fairly modern (150–200 years old), which should be retained. Tree planting and recreational development should be in the three arable fields. The mix of tree species should be as natural as possible and designed to enhance the ecology of the site, but this need not preclude a small percentage of trees chosen for amenity interest.

There should also be provision for recreation, both formal (for example a golf driving range) and informal (for example footpaths and picnic areas). The edges of these areas should be graded from short grass, through to meadow grass, shrubs and understorey to provide a range of ecological niches outside of any closed canopy woodland. Parts of the woodland may be high forest and open canopy with dense understorey, possibly to include areas for coppicing.

There is no requirement for a harvestable timber crop, but we would like to have the potential to provide raw material for rural crafts, and any amenity and landscape trees should be chosen so that should they need to be felled, there is value in their timber.

Money is short so proposals that are low in cost or draw in resources from other sources (grants, sponsorship etc) would be welcome.

The college requires that the students' report should at least contain: a statement of aims and objectives; proposals for woodland development; a description of how these proposals would be implemented or encouraged. This should include some presentation of the economics of the plan, particularly sources of resources.

Students are judged on the inventiveness, feasibility and suitability of the plan, their recognition of possible problems and opportunities and their understanding of the role which trees can play in addressing their objectives.

Learning resources
Of the three case studies featured below, only the Farming and Conservation in the 1990s package was designed for use in the FHE sector. Nevertheless, the Hypertext training materials designed to assist farmers are highly relevant to any future pesticide user. Similarly, although the Landscapes for Tomorrow project was designed to educate and engage the public in landscape planning, the envisioning process used is highly relevant to environmental policy-making in general and, in turn, to those likely to be involved in it in the future.

A common feature of all three resources is their emphasis on the learner/player interacting with information/data/images in order to come to his/her own conclusions in relation to appropriate actions. This emphasis is in keeping with the 'deep' approach to learning.

IT Learning Package: farming and conservation in the 1990s,
developed by English Nature in partnership with the Royal
Agricultural College, Cirencester

This pack has been designed to explore ways in which nature conservation and environmental principles can be integrated into farming. It uses

two real farms of different types – a lowland arable and a mixed upland.
The complete pack consists of:

- 32 page introductory booklet on how to use the pack;

- computer disk containing the workshop pack on Bryn Garth Farm
  and Melbury Farm;

- pack of 20 colour transparency slides, 10 for each farm;

- set of 8 overhead transparencies, 4 for each farm;

- A4 colour plan for each farm;

- 4 A4 maps showing protected areas in England, Scotland and Wales;

- computer disk containing a comprehensive environmental information database.

*Hypertext Training Materials for Rational Pesticide Use, developed
by Southampton University*

Pesticide use surveys, carried out by Southampton's Agrochemicals
Evaluation Unit (EAU), have revealed that over-spraying is common, and
that at least 100,000 hectares in the UK were receiving broad-spectrum
insecticides leading to pest resurgence, low profits and in some cases,
financial loss. Rational pesticide use can be summarised as using the correct
pesticide, at the correct time, in the correct place and in the correct way.
The benefits of observing these rules are not just environmental, but also
economic. This is of particular concern to those involved in the agrochemical
industries as well as the users. Of particular importance is the principle
of spraying the crop at the correct time, which can be determined by a
process of forecasting pest outbreaks.

The EAU developed an interactive computer system to guide farmers
in the rational use of pesticides on arable crops. This system was made
available through Hoechst UK on telephone/modem (Hoechst Agrochemical
Enquiry Viewdata System) to more than a million hectares of arable land
in the UK. It was run on the Hoechst UK main frame via a view data system
for farmers. It poses a number of questions to the farmer which relate to
the stage of growth of the crop, the level of pest infestation and the market
the farmer is aiming at. In response, the software offers appropriate advice
on whether or not to spray. It also assists farmers to calculate the reductions
in profits likely from using pesticides unnecessarily.

Following on from this pilot, a training need was identified in order to improve understanding of the concept of pest thresholds and rational pesticide use, facilitate the confident and informed use of advisory software. And with the support of the European Commission through a COMETT grant, a project team was set up to develop hypertext materials.

The interactive hypertext incorporates pest control advisory software, together with visual and textual information to train farmers in the concepts underlying the methods of rational pesticide management. These materials were selected for inclusion in the exhibition of European Commission training materials at the 1992 Hanover Trade Fair. They were also selected by the European Task Force for Human Resources for consideration at the 1993 conference concerning agricultural training needs and the reformed CAP. The software has been widely used for training throughout the European Union. The hypertext materials were developed by Dr Steve Wratten, formerly at Southampton University, now at Wellington College, New Zealand, and Dr Allen Pritchard and Phil McNulty of Phoenix European Programmes.

Landscapes for Tomorrow: a Participatory Exercise in Landscape Interpretation developed by the University of East Anglia and the Yorkshire Dales National Park (O'Riordan, Wood and Shandrake 1992)

Countryside interpretation in the UK tends to be a static and passive exercise. The emphasis has been on explaining features or events, rather than addressing issues. Displays are fixed and the visiting public are expected to read and absorb. What people think and how they react to the images provided, particularly if choices are involved, remains largely unexplored.

The aim of the Landscapes for Tomorrow Project was to assess the extent to which an innovative package of interpretive experiences could stimulate the public to travel along a pathway that embraced four objectives. These were:

i.   to develop understanding by informing;

ii. to increase awareness by linking information to individual feelings about future landscapes;

iii. to generate concern for the protection, enhancement and re-creation of dales landscapes;

iv. to stimulate a desire to become involved in landscape planning.

Two travelling exhibitions were visited by 15,000 people during the Autumn of 1989 and summer of 1990. The exhibitions contained visual displays of how landscapes in the Yorkshire Dales had altered in the past, together with the pictorial images of seven possible future landscapes. Based on the same scene, the landscapes showed how the countryside might look according to different, but equally plausible, changes in agriculture and regional economic and landscape planning policy.

In order to introduce an element of personal discovery into the exhibition, a game of choices was devised. The game is based on a walk through an imaginary dale. As players progress along the route (by shaking a dice) messages have to be absorbed and choices made concerning individual landscape features – walls, meadows, barns, trees and moors. The sum total of a player's choices result in a future landscape of the players own making, which may or may not differ from the seven futures depicted by the research team.

The evaluation of participants' experience showed that imagining landscape futures is a powerful approach to interpretation. Of particular significance was that many participants felt that the experience of the exhibit now made them better equipped, confident and motivated to influence future planning/management decisions concerning dales landscapes of the twenty-first century.

Training and advice
As cross-curricular provision improves, the shape of updating provision will change. Because the existing workforce has not received a basic environmental education, updating will for some time need to cover first principles as well as new discoveries, techniques and legislation.

Training and advisory services working in partnership with practitioners are uniquely placed to assess whether environmental education principles translate into practice and to assess the effectiveness of environmental education approaches. The training resources, strategies and codes of practice developed by MAFF, Agricultural and Development Advisory Service, the Agricultural Training Board, the Countryside Commission, the Farmers and Wildlife Advisory Group, English Nature, the National Farmers Union and a whole range of environmental non-governmental organisations are rich sources of the latest thinking about the promotion of sustainable practice in relation to rural sector activity. These resources should inform curriculum development and pedagogy.

Research
The central argument in this publication is that all rural sector courses should be set in their appropriate environmental context. So too should

all rural sector research projects. The suggestion is that the direction of research, research questions and recommendations based on research findings should take appropriate account of the environment.

As regards specialist research there is a need for more research into sustainable land management. This should include basic research into resource conserving technologies in a wide variety of biophysical and socio-economic contexts and action research in relation to current practice (Pretty *et al*, 1993). It is also important for research findings to inform both curriculum development and practice. Indeed, there is a need for better information flows between all actors within the rural sector.

The following two case studies are illustrative of current research areas, namely the integrated farming model and environmental auditing in arable agriculture.

International Institute for Environment and Development (IIED): Research Series of the Sustainable Agriculture Programme

This series reports the findings of collaborative research carried out as part of the programme's activities. Each volume is devoted to a different research project.

The Policies for Resource Conserving Agriculture project is investigating the economic and environmental viability of alternatives to industrialised, conventional or Green Revolution agriculture in selected countries of the Third World, the UK and Europe, and the US. It is drawing on cases of successful application of resource conserving practices and systems, elucidating the components of success and developing policy frameworks to encourage alternative agriculture.

One report coming out of this project is 'Sustainable Agriculture in Britain: Recent Achievements and New Policy Challenges' (Pretty *et al*, 1993). The report emphasises the economic and environmental viability of the integrated farming model. The characteristics of this model include a more thorough integration of natural processes into the agricultural production process, combined with a reduction in the use of off-farm inputs, to achieve profitable and efficient production. This model does not constitute a return to low technology or low output, and is not a single system of technologies and practices. It includes a wide spectrum of farming systems involving prudent use of pesticides, antibiotics and fertilisers. Conventional practices are not rejected, but the innovative resource-conserving practices are emphasised. These usually involve the substitution of labour, knowledge and management skills for the former high use of external inputs.

Within the report, detailed tables of evidence are presented to illustrate that integrated farms can match or better the gross margins of conventional farming, even though there is usually a yield per hectare reduction of some 5–10 per cent for crops and 10–20 per cent for livestock.

MAFF-funded Research Project: Environmental Auditing in Arable Agriculture

The key objectives of this project are to:

i.   facilitate a technical system for environmental auditing to be applied to arable agriculture and related livestock enterprises (that this, intensive poultry and pig units);

ii.   develop the technical details of a PC-based system which can be made available to farmers to improve environmental performance in application areas and to examine the potential of an expert system in this context;

iii. pilot, validate and evaluate outcomes in terms of, for example, changed attitudes and practices in a variety of settings.

The approach adopted consists of first reviewing environmental auditing in a broad economic and international context, and then devising applicable environmental auditing methods and developing a technical system to allow application to agriculture. Third, database analysis and appropriate specialist consultations are required to allow system development and calibration. Finally, piloting in a variety of contexts (research and commercial farms) needs to be undertaken in order to examine 'workability' and to evaluate outcomes, in particular to assess the system as a tool to widen the uptake of the Codes of Good Agricultural Practice.

This three-year project is a joint initiative between the University of Hertfordshire, Rothampsted Experimental Station, A D Advisory Service, and SWRC.

3   INTEGRATION METHODS

Cross-curricular greening is a large and complex task. There is no model to emulate, indeed since course structures vary from one institution to another and course curricula may be subject to nationally determined criteria, a national model would be inappropriate. In addition, the size of the environmental component will vary.

There are various ways of delivering environmental education to students taking non environmental courses. The few institutions experimenting in this area are at a very early stage of implementation. However the strengths and weaknesses of the different approaches are beginning to emerge.

3.1   Modular Approaches

Modular course structures provide a useful framework for building environmental education into students' learning programmes. Some institutions now offer optional environmental modules. The disadvantage of this 'cafeteria approach' to environmental education is that it is difficult to ensure that students get a 'square-meal'.

Optional modules
Optional modules, which may be available to students from several courses, often cover generic environmental education themes. A criticism of this type of module relates to perceived relevance. An optional module which covers the principles of sustainability, for instance, but which does not make connections with the student's own chosen area of study tends to be perceived at best as interesting but peripheral, and at worst irrelevant. Such modules need to be customised for particular courses.

Relevance
The student's perception of what is relevant also poses problems for introducing environmental education for personal responsibility. Where courses include a customised module relating to environmental education for occupational responsibility, the personal links can be made in the context of environmental themes relevant to the student's chosen course, thereby maintaining relevance. There is a need for creative thinking as regards delivery of environmental education for personal responsibility, which might include a strategy to change students' perception about the relevance of this area of provision.

Very little research has been carried out to evaluate which environmental education approaches best meet the fundamental objective of environmental education, which is to encourage sustainable practice. It may be that enabling a personal commitment to sustainable practice is a prerequisite for an equivalent occupational commitment.

Compulsory customised module

The compulsory customised module is preferable to the optional module since it enables a planned approach to the introduction of appropriate environmental education elements and because connections to students' own courses can be made. The compulsory nature of this type of module can present problems in cases where the curriculum is already crowded. The compulsory introduction of an environmental module could mean the loss of another part of the course. Some courses, in particular those whose curricula are externally determined, may be unable to accommodate an environmental module.

The appropriateness of a compulsory environmental module also depends on the whether the course has significant environmental implications. For instance, rural environment courses would have significant environmental implications. The inclusion of one or more modules would therefore be appropriate. In the case of courses with very few environmental connections an environmental module may be inappropriate.

Bolt-on

The major criticism of the modular route to cross-curricular greening is its 'bolt-on' nature, which encourages the compartmentalisation of environmental concerns. However, supporters of the use of specific environmental modules as a route to integration argue that students are capable of making their own connections with other course modules.

Well planned, occupationally targeted environmental modules have proved a useful way of introducing environmental components into a wide range of rural courses. It may be necessary for environmental themes to be reinforced in a variety of ways during a course. The emphasis is on producing environmentally literate and competent graduates and diplomates, and there is no 'correct' or 'tried and tested' best way of doing this. It is necessary for institutions to experiment.

3.2   Student Projects

Environment-related projects across all disciplines are a useful vehicle for integration whatever the course structure. They have the potential to:

- enable students to bring their own environmental concerns to the environmental education agenda, since many projects offer students flexibility of topic choice;

- increase the environmental awareness of staff and thus encourage course revision;

- create a demand for appropriate library resources;

- enable the greening of institutional practice through specific pieces of research, marketing exercises and practical tasks;

- enable the development of lifeskills/active citizenship skills which are regarded as part of quality learning, through working on 'live' issues;

- offer an opportunity for students to work in partnership, for example with employers, non-governmental organisations, or staff and students from other institutions, and through this to develop team skills.

Environmental projects may be regarded as an important part of any environmental education strategy.

3.3   Experiential Learning

Experiential learning is particularly important in relation to attitudinal and behavioural aspects of the environmental education agenda. Students can learn useful behavioural lessons within their institutions, for instance, by participating in their institution's recycling scheme or adhering to its environmental policies relating to the efficient use of paper.

Experiential learning outside the institution would include a whole range of activities; for example, local visits. These may include visits to local sites which are noted for their natural beauty or ecological interest but which are the focus of an environmental conflict. This would then encourage an understanding of local environmental limits and strategies to keep within those limits.

Experimental learning could also include field research. Examples of field research include: an attitudinal survey, for instance to a local development; a species survey; an investigation of pollution levels in local water courses due to fertiliser and pesticide run-off; and an investigation of waste management patterns in the horticultural industry. In other words, field research extends beyond its traditional definition relating to threatened sites of particular ecological value.

Placements are also of value in experiential learning. Some courses include a placement scheme. They are extremely effective both in opening students' eyes to the opportunities available, and in opening employers' eyes to student capabilities. In terms of the environment a placement can be a teaching and learning experience for both employer and employee. It can assist in the integration of employers' environmental knowledge and skills being fed back into the curriculum by the student, and the integration of the students' environmental knowledge and skills ideas into the workplace.

The DfE 'Environmental Responsibility' (1993) report recommends that specialist environmental courses (which we can also take to mean courses with significant environmental implications) which do not at present offer placements should seriously consider doing so.

Experiential learning relating to the environment also encourages environmental appreciation. This is often thought of in terms of the beauty of the environment. However, it is often only when something is lost, or almost lost, that its value is appreciated. As such environmental appreciation may come from viewing both beautiful and degraded environments.

In addition environmental appreciation goes beyond aesthetics. For instance, field work develops an appreciation of environmental utility or loss of utility, biological diversity or loss of diversity, balance or imbalance, and can encourage students to value the environment.

Placing a value on the environment is the first step towards developing a commitment to active environmental citizenship, since duties and obligations stem from values. While first-hand experience is conducive to an appreciation of the value of the environment, there are other ways of encouraging environmental appreciation. It may be developed through 'interpreters' – artists, singers, poets, visionary speakers. For example, beautiful landscapes may be appreciated, albeit not in the same way as if seen personally, through landscape paintings; the loss of a species may be appreciated through a poem; the diversity of species may be appreciated through a nature programme on television.

3.4   Environmental Learning Outcomes

Environmental learning outcomes are an expression of the level of environmental competence students are expected to achieve at the end of their course. They are a useful starting point for developing a coordinated strategy for the inclusion of appropriate environmental education elements within a course and provide a focus for an assessment strategy. Please see BTEC learning outcome series (Ali Khan, 1992).

4   EVALUATION METHODS

Today evaluation means, at least in part, performance indicators. Returning to an earlier theme it is important that institutional commitment and performance is evaluated, as well as more specific curriculum activities. The following series of indicators has been endorsed by Professor Peter Toyne, the chair of the Department for Education's committee which produced the 'Environmental Responsibility' report.

Environmental Responsibility Indicators: Institutional and Academic Practice

• Comprehensive environmental policy statement for both institutional and academic practice

• Strategy for implementing the institution's environmental policy

• Environmental advisory group to guide strategy implementation

• Accreditation to BS 7750 or similar mechanism for systematically managing the institution's environmental responsibilities

• Annual environmental audit/environmental performance report

Environmental Responsibility Indicators: Academic Practice

• Framework for cross-curricular, environmental education including learning outcomes relevant to all students and learning outcomes relating to specific educational areas (NB: these may include those identified by professional/examining bodies).

• List of current in-house expertise in relation to the environment

• Staff development programme relating to the institution's environmental education framework, for example programme summary, number of staff involved, time commitment

• Institution membership of/formal links with environmental professional bodies, agencies or organisations (local, national and international)

• List of criteria used for internal assessment of cross-curricular environmental education provision

- Accreditation or assessment report of cross-curricular environmental education provision by external body, for example professional body or independent assessor

- Student survey report relating to awareness of institution's environmental policy and satisfaction with environmental education provision

- Employer satisfaction survey report relating to the environmental competence of named recruits to named companies/organisations, from named courses

REFERENCES

Ali Khan, S. (1992) 'Colleges Going Green: A Guide to Environmental Action in Further Education Colleges' (London: Further Education Unit).

Ali Khan, S. (1992) 'BTEC Environmental Initiative' (London: BTEC).

Compassion in World Farming Trust (1993) *The Welfare of Pigs, Cattle and Sheep at Slaughter* (Hants: Compassion in World Farming).

Council for Occupational Standards and Qualifications in Environmental Conservation (1994) 'Environmental Integrity of Occupational Standards (Gloucester).

Countryside Commission (1989) 'Training for Tomorrow's Countryside: Report of the Countryside Staff Training Advisory Group', CCPCCP 269 (Cheltenham).

Dearing, R. (1994) *The National Curriculum and its Assessment: Final Report* (London: School and Assessment Authority).

Department for Education (1992) 'Environmental Responsibility: An Agenda for Further and Higher Education' (London: HMSO).

Duke of Westminster (1992) 'The Problems in Rural Areas' (Brecon, Powys).

European Commission (1992) *Fifth Environmental Action Programme* (Brussels: European Commission).

Gibb, G. (1992) *Improving the Quality of Student Learning*, (Council for National Academic Awards, Technical and Educational Services Ltd).

HMI (1991) 'The Response of Agricultural Colleges to Changing Needs', London: Department for Education and Science.

O'Riordan, T. (1993) 'Towards Sustainable Futures' in *On the Fringe of the Machine: Annual Review of Environmental Education*, (Reading: Council for Environmental Education).

O'Riordan, T., Wood, C. and Shadrake, A. (1992) *Landscapes for Tomorrow: A Participatory Exercise in Landscape Interpretation* (Yorkshire Dales National Park).

Pretty, J.N. & Howes, R. (1993) *Sustainable Agriculture in Britain: Recent Achievements and New Policy Challenges*, International Institute for Environment and Development (IIED) Research Series, Volume 2, No. 1 (London: IIED).

Royal Society for the Protection of Birds (1991) 'Conservation Education in Colleges of Agriculture' (Sandy: RSPB).

Royal Society for the Protection of Birds (1993) 'The Environment Factor: Developing an Environmental Programme in Further and Higher Education' (Sandy: RSPB).

'Sustainable Development: the UK Strategy' (HMSO: 1994).

United Nations Conference on Environment and Development (UNCED) (1992) *Agenda 21* (New York: UN).

SERIES BIBLIOGRAPHY

Ali Khan S, 1992, *BTEC Environmental Initiative*, BTEC, London.

Ali Khan S, 1992, *Colleges Going Green: A Guide to Environmental Action in Further Education Colleges*, Further Education Unit, London.

Centre for Human Ecology, University of Edinburgh, 'Environmental Education for Adaptation', November 1991.

Committee of Directors of Polytechnics, 'Greening Polytechnics', October 1990.

Committee of Directors of Polytechnics, 'Greening the Curriculum', May 1991.

Committee of Vice Chancellors and Principals, 'Universities & the Environment: Environmental Regulation – Opportunities & Obligations', February 1992.

Department for Education, 1993, *Environmental Responsibility: An Agenda for Further and Higher Education*, HMSO, London.

Government White Paper on the Environment, 'This Common Inheritance', HMSO, September 1990.

Institution of Environmental Sciences, *Environmental Education in Higher Education*, Position Paper, 1994.

National Curriculum Council, 'Environmental Education', *Curriculum Guidance* 7, 1990.

Scottish Environmental Education Council, 'Towards Environmental Competence in Scotland: An Overview', November 1991.